THE
DESIGNER'S
WAY:

Designing HER Way to Happy in the Second Half of Life

A GUIDEBOOK FOR 'BECOMING' AS WE AGE

by Linda Jensen, MA. Ed.S. Design Your Life Coach

Balboa Press books may be ordered through booksellers or by contacting:

Balboa Press
A Division of Hay House
1663 Liberty Drive
Bloomington, IN 47403
www.balboapress.com
844-682-1282

Because of the dynamic nature of the Internet, any web addresses or links contained in this book may have changed since publication and may no longer be valid. The views expressed in this work are solely those of the author and do not necessarily reflect the views of the publisher, and the publisher hereby disclaims any responsibility for them.

Any people depicted in stock imagery provided by Getty Images are models, and such images are being used for illustrative purposes only.
Certain stock imagery © Getty Images.

ISBN: 978-1-9822-6268-6 (sc)
ISBN: 978-1-9822-6269-3 (e)

Print information available on the last page.

Balboa Press rev. date: 02/06/2021

BALBOA.PRESS
A DIVISION OF HAY HOUSE

CONTENTS

Introducing the DESIGNER'S WAY: This guidebook is written for women 50 and forward with an inner craving to become and express our best self now that we have completed the journey through the first half of life. It is our time to 'become' meaning it is time to step into our true self and our true spirit to meet our grit and live our grace. The DESIGNER'S WAY is my way to guide this journey back to you-the true you- the core you so that you become your best self and live a best life for the rest of your life.

I am Linda Jensen a Design Your Life Coach for *Women 50 and Forward.* My undergraduate and graduate degrees are in Psychology. While not using this knowledge base as a clinical psychologist, I have applied it in my career as a School Psychologist, Director of Special Education for a school district, Director of Pediatrics for a rehab hospital, Project Director for several large child welfare grants, and as a State Director for a child advocacy organization. In each of these positions, my career passion was to find and create ways to help vulnerable children and families have the access to the resources and support they needed to reach their full potential. My Encore Passion NOW is to empower women in reaching their potential to thrive in the second half of life. To this end, I have become a Certified Design Your Life Coach from both Stanford University and the Life Purpose Institute. This passion for Life Design evolved through social innovation work using Design Thinking as my solution development model. Design Thinking is a human centered approach that brings the potential user to the forefront of the planning process. My personalized Life Design Coaching model combines Design Thinking, Thought Biology, Personality Type, and Adult Female Development Theory into an approach I call the Designer's Way. This process follows the steps of Discover, Define, Dream, Decide, Develop, and Dance to arrive at an Encore Career or Encore Life Plan designed to become an Encore

Performance for good. In other words, my Encore Performance is to help women design their Encore Performance.

After retiring early and finding myself bored, restless, and frustrated that I had become my best self, but didn't have a satisfying way to express myself, I began a reflective journey. This journey explored: who I am at my core nature; who I am as a Boomer Gen woman; who I have become from a strength perspective; who I want to be now; how I want to be now and why. This reflective process motivated my decision to use my passion for empowerment, design, and psychology to become a Design Your Life Coach and create a unique online six-week Designing Your Encore Life 'Design and Do' Lab Package designed to help women become their grit in the second half of life.

The components of this lab include:

- Online Six-Week Designing Your Encore 'Design and Do' Lab

- Life Design Workbook

- Weekly Mastermind Group for Coaching Support, Networking, and Radical Collaboration

The Designer's Way process follows the steps of:

- **Discover:** The 'True You'

- **Define:** What you want and why

- **Dream:** Imagine all ways possible

- **Decide:** Set a new direction

- **Develop**: Create an Action Plan for success

- **Dance:** Manifest your new reality

This unique online Life Coaching package is available for purchase at **encoredesignherlife.com**

Understanding Women in the Second Half of Life

As women in the second half of life, we are in a unique position to create change based on life experiences and the wisdom we have derived from it. We are also in a unique position to create change based on our biology. Science reveals that women have a leg up physically in the aging process in that they experience new brain growth after the age of 50. The only other time this happens is during the teen years. This growth takes place in the temporal lobe identified with emotional learning. New growth is in Myelin, the fatty substance that insulates and speeds up connection between nerve cells. The outcome is an enhanced ability to make good judgment calls. The brain works in ways that stimulate a new stage of understanding and accomplishment. These psychological advantages play out in a variety of strengths: mental strengths to solve problems; identity strengths to manage role changes that come with aging; relational strengths that build compassion and caring; emotional strengths to manage hardship and crisis that can happen more often as we get older. These strengths allow a mindset in which we can celebrate older age as a time of Fun, Freedom, and Fulfillment. This brain growth facilitates behavior changes like:

- Shedding the 'Shoulds' to get to 'Musts'

- Letting go of Limiting Beliefs

- Using your personality in new ways to get to your Best Self NOW

- Using your potential in new ways to effect change

- Redefining power to mean love- power comes from what you love and what you love gives you power

Research also confirms a developmental reality between men and women as they age. Adult males start from a grounding in Active Mastery and tend to move towards a state of Passive Mastery whereas, women tend to start from a grounding in Passive Mastery characterized by dependence and responsibility and move in later life towards Active Mastery. This allows them to become more independent, autonomous, effective, self-confident, and ultimately more powerful.

Developmentally, women in the second half of life want to use their voice to empower others to find their voice. Their ambition moves towards self-fulfillment; their need for recognition is replaced by self-confidence; their personal success overrides achievement; knowing is replaced by learning new things. Gail Sheehy, in her book 'Passages', describes the developmental stages of women in the second half of life as follows:

- **The Fifties:** A time when we begin to search for meaning and move on from the idea of pleasing others, to asserting our own mastery.

- **The Sixties:** A time to experience maximum freedom even though we begin to deal with physical limitations. It is also when we prioritize our values and sense of purpose as we gain confidence in knowing that we will be loved for who we have become.

- **The Seventies:** A time of growth and development as we become our own masters. This empowers us as capable mediators and mentors for others. We must commit ourselves to growth or we risk drifting into passivity and despair.

- **The Eighties & Nineties:** The challenge is to resist being overwhelmed with negativity. It's imperative that we look inside ourselves for courage and stay focused on enjoying the benefits of life.

After decades in the workforce and in the trenches fighting for human rights and social change, women in the second half of life are not ready to retire to the golf course or the rocking chair on the front porch. These Gen Z and Boomer Gen women are determined to put their experience to work in new ways to empower and create meaningful change. As the nation confronts significant challenges in the areas of education, environment, income inequality, and immigration (to name a few), a windfall of second act talent could help propel us towards a new generation of ideas for change.

Transition is a developmental phenomenon for most *Women 50 and Forward*. Life transitions such as moving into or thinking about retirement can be an exciting and invigorating time in life but, these changes can also be stressful. How we view transitions determines how we manage challenges. Transitions often force us to adapt to different life situations that can challenge our sense of identity. Some transitions call upon us to change our values and with that, how we act. In each of the transitions we make, we must tune into our emerging selves. As women, we need to understand our previous and current identity and dig deep to discover the authentic, essential self that wants a voice now. We can only let go of past or broken stories when we can imagine new and better ones. Part of the process of transition is leaving behind certain dreams, beliefs, and concerns we consider important so that we can allow ourselves space for new modified dreams and beliefs to emerge. Reframing transition to see new ways to manage challenge is key to moving through the transition process. Mid-life transition issues can include retirement, loss of spouse, empty nest, relocation, health issues, etc.

In mid-life, Legacy also starts to become top of mind. We begin to think about leaving a part of ourselves behind after we are gone. Legacy is about how we want to be remembered. It's about learning from the past, living in the present, and building for the future. Legacy is fundamental to what it is to be human. Research shows that without a sense of working to create a Legacy, adults lose meaning in their life. Exploring the idea of Legacy offers insight, not only into how you want to be remembered, but also reveals who you are as a human spirit. In the end, Legacy is about the things we love and value most. It is about how we become our grit.

Women and Mastery in the Second Half of Life

I am a woman in the second half of life. I'm not finished trying to make a difference. I see myself as a designer first and foremost. I love the process of designing interiors, landscapes, and social innovation programs. I am now using my design skills to help women design their lives.

My life design process works to help women find their true self in mid to later life. True self looks like discovering, uncovering, and expressing Passion, Purpose, and Power in ways that convey mastery. Mastery begins with knowing who you are as a soul. Who you are as a soul is who you are at your core. Who you are at your core is the 'True You' wanting to find your own sense of Passion, Purpose, and Power NOW in the second half of life. I am convinced that the world is in its' current state of chaos because women have not been empowered enough to know and manifest their own sense of mastery. The world needs us to stand in our power now. The world needs us to recommit to making a difference, but on our own terms. We have earned our time for leisure. We have earned our time for self-reflection. We have earned our time for adventure, and we have earned our time to love deeply without feeling responsible for others happiness. But, there is a longing for meaning and fulfillment. There is a longing to find our own way home. Home is who we are as women who have become masters of our own destiny.

Now that I have arrived at the age I am, I feel close to mastering my destiny. I know who I am, and I know how I want to spend the next years of my life. I am learning to dance to my own rhythm. I am learning to find Fun, Freedom, and Fulfillment in later life, and I want to help others do the same.

What does Fun, Freedom, and Fulfillment look like to you NOW? I hope you take the time to investigate this question, because it will be well worth your time. Using my program

'Designing Your Encore Life', is one way to do this. We all want to find new ways to enjoy life. We all want to find new ways to have the freedom to be our 'True Self'. We all want to find new ways to find meaning and fulfillment. Fulfillment is a byproduct of mastery. Mastery is a byproduct of living the life your soul intended. You living the life your soul intended, is you finding and expressing your Passion, Purpose, and Power NOW. Passion, Purpose, and Power mean different things to different people. Passion is what you love at your core. It is what brings you to tears when you think about it. It is what creates meaning in life. I have a passion for HALO Girls. This is my own acronym for High Ability, Low Opportunity. I so admire girls who have the grit to work through their challenges in a way that inspires them to become leaders and changemakers. I am contributing a portion of my book profits to support organizations that empower HALO Girls. Purpose is when you find a way to express your passion. It is about the way forward. Power is you standing up for who you are and what you believe. Power is you being YOU at your core. Power is reframing the idea of challenge to see opportunity.

Now that we have arrived at the second half of life, it important to examine who we were in the first half of life. As women, we must take a deep dive into our past to understand how past experience has impacted our sense of self now. We are a generation of women who equate the word power with conflict. Some of our generation came of age during World War II. Others came of age during the Vietnam War, while others came of age during the civil rights conflict. War and fighting was how we learned to view conflict. This view translates easily into our approach to solving life problems now. I can become a fighter when I am pushed, but I see women as having the brain power to solve problems without war. I see that our experience and our wisdom become even more useful in conflict resolution as we age.

How does our view of conflict impact who we want to become in the second half of life? It creates a mindset for how we act. I want to see opportunity in challenge. I want to face my aging with grit and grace, and work to avoid feeling the fear that comes with challenge but, I also want to continue to fight for the values I believe in. I love the quote by Nelson Mandela "When you fight for what you believe in, you fight for yourself". I want to help women fight for themselves in ways that change both them and our world. How does this happen? First, we need to come to the conclusion that women in the second half of life have value. Then, we need to understand that we have power. Power comes from the knowledge that wisdom matters. The world needs our power and our wisdom to bring us back to a state of 'We'. 'We' is knowing what is good for me is good for you and what is good for you is good for me. I continually work to build my understanding of how my thoughts drive my reactions to conflict. If I step back and take a broader view of how I can reframe my conflict to see opportunity, I can move away from 'Me' to a state of 'We'. An example for me is the inherent conflict in the concept of aging. I can view aging as a fight to the finish or I can reframe it to see opportunity to find news ways to express my Passion, Purpose, and Power NOW. I can view it as a time to become a compassionate warrior, to fight for the kind of change that creates a better 'We'. To me, a compassionate warrior is a woman in the second half of life who becomes her grit to fight for social justice, human rights, and self.

As *Women 50 and Forward*, most of us are seeking ways to become masters of our own destiny. I look for ways to make sense of my life story and the challenges included in it. I want to figure out how challenge can inspire opportunity for personal growth. Women are hardwired to find opportunity in challenge. We are hardwired to be problem-solvers. We are hardwired to use our talents, skills, and abilities to make a difference. We are at our prime as compassionate warriors. Women in the second half of life are also at their prime to become masters. Mastery is a mindset. We are all working to become masters of our own destiny. My destiny feels like working with women who along with me are trying to understand their destiny. Now that I am a Life Coach, I have created the Designer's Way to help women find their destiny in the second half of life.

Step 1: Discover- The 'True You'

Discovering passion and purpose starts with discovering who you are as an individual. Discovering who you are as an individual starts with discovering who you are as a personality. Personality Type defines how we live and how we age. Personality Type is who you are as a biological entity. It is the hardwiring you were born with. It is the DNA that you brought into the world. Your Personality Type reflects your core nature. I like to use the Myers Briggs Personality Type Test to help clients determine their Personality Type. It assesses the personality preferences of:

- **Extraversion (E) and Introversion (I):** This pair refers to where we prefer to focus our attention and what energizes us.

- **Sensing (S) and Intuiting (N):** This pair refers to how we prefer to take in information.

- **Thinking (T) and Feeling (F):** This pair refers to how we evaluate information and make decisions.

- **Judging (J) and Perceiving (P):** This pair refers to our lifestyle orientation.

Learning your Personality Type can help you understand the life you have led and help you guide the new life you want to design now. A key takeaway from taking the Myers Briggs Personality Type Test at this stage of life, is understanding whether you fall into the Thinker or Feeler category. Feelers are people who want to experience life from the inside. Thinkers are people who experience life by reacting to external forces and environments. Feelers like to know they are making a difference in the way people feel. Thinkers like to know they are making a difference in how people respond. As a Feeler in the second half of life, I want to help people feel like life is worth living. I want to help women understand that in the second half life they have arrived at their best self and that the world needs them now to express themselves in a way that makes them happy, while also serving the greater good. I want to help women feel their power to serve the greater good. Thinkers bring logic to the second half of life. They want to help others make sense of their life now. Thinkers find ways to enjoy the later stage of life in a way that manages life for the best possible outcomes. Thinkers also want to help others make their lives have meaning through outcomes. Most people are a combination of both feeler and thinker but have a preference that drives their decision-making. My role as a Life Coach is to help clients find strength in their preference and develop a sense of 'True Self' that motivates the design for a new life going forward.

As mentioned earlier, the way the Myers Briggs Personality Type Indicator works is to assess the contrast of Introversion vs. Extroversion; Sensing vs. Intuiting; Feeling vs. Thinking; Perception vs. Judging to arrive at a four-letter type that explains why you are who you are. These types become a good indicator of how we will age. My type is INFP. This means that I am an introverted woman who thinks about what I say before I say it. It also means that I am intuitive in a way that brings awareness of my surroundings and how they influence my actions and behaviors. Intuitive personalities think deeply and care deeply. As a Feeler, I measure success by the way others feel. My own sense of success has a lot to do with how others make me feel. I do not want my feelings to rule my life, so I work hard to understand and reframe them.

When you understand Personality Type, you can begin to think about how your type can be expressed to your advantage in the second half of life. You can think about how it can become your compass as you age. Here are examples of how each of the 16 Personality Types express themselves in the second half of life. Again, the preference options are Extroversion (E) vs. Introversion (I); Sensing (S) vs. Intuitive (N); Thinking (T) vs. Feeling (F); Judging (J) vs. Perception (P).

- **ISTJ:** We want to continue to make a difference as we grow older. We look for new ways to influence outcomes for groups and causes we care about.

- **INFP:** We are deep thinkers and deep feelers. We are motivated to go the extra mile to create change in ways that empower society and humanity.

- **ISTJ:** We are women who like things to be orderly and well executed. We work to organize our environments in ways that create better and more efficient systems and effect meaningful change.

- **INTJ**: We are women who care about how our actions and behaviors impact outcomes.

- **INFJ:** We are thinkers who are willing to go out on a limb to make things right. We care deeply, but are cautious about taking risks. As women in the second half of life, we like to manage our environments and look for ways to help others we care about.

- **INTP:** We are women who work for justice. We work to find solutions for social issues we care about. As older women, we like to get involved in organizations that are social justice based.

- **ISTP:** We are women who want to share their knowledge. We are the teachers of the world. As older women we continue to be involved as volunteer teachers.

- **ISFP**: We are women who want to save the earth. We care about climate change and we care about how our behavior impacts our environment. As older women, we continue to want to support these causes.

- **ISTJ**: We are bookworms. We read to learn about people. We read to learn about the environment, and we read to learn about ourselves. As women in the second half of life we have great knowledge to share.

- **ENFP:** We are outgoing and friendly. We love people and want to be social. We work to find ways to connect. As women in the second half of life we are motivated to bring people together to solve problems.

- **ESFP**: We like people who are like us. We work to find like-minded women to share activities and interests in common. We are feelers and look for ways to help others.

- **ESTJ:** We are women who organize and advocate for issues we care about. We look for ways to make the world a better place to live. As women in the second half of life we look for ways to connect with groups that support causes and issues we care about.

- **ENFP:** We are women who are socially motivated to join and create groups that serve our internal drives. We are women who are likely to be project directors for organizations that serve populations and causes we care about. As women in the second half of life we still want to be leaders and changemakers.

- **ENTP:** We are women who are still movers, shakers, and changemakers. As women in the second half of life we are the doers for projects for work or volunteering.

- **ESFJ:** We are the ones that feel our way to action. We don't like to feel bad, so we work to manage our environment to avoid conflict. As we age, we look for ways to keep the peace and avoid conflict.

- **ENTJ:** We are thinkers who go inside to find our answers. We want to help others find their answers and seek ways to teach them how to find their way in life.

- **ENFJ:** We are women who feel our way home. We have an internal drive to understand the meaning of life and like to meet in groups to discuss our views. As women in the second half of life, finding meaning and making sense of life becomes even more important.

Knowing your Personality Type provides a framework for finding and understanding your Passion and Purpose NOW in the second half of life. As an INFP in later life, I continue to feel through design. I still love interior and landscape design and now have a passion for life design. This passion is expressed by helping women design their way to happy in the second half of life. My purpose is to help them find meaning and purpose at this stage of life. Purpose can be an abstract thing.

What does purpose have to do with how you want to live now? Sense of purpose has everything to do with what you want going forward. Purpose speaks to what happy looks like. Purpose looks like fulfillment. Discovering purpose helps define the 'True You' that wants expression now in the second half of life.

Potential is an expression of passion and purpose. How you express your passion and purpose depends on how you understand your potential. Potential is a combination of your hardwiring/personality type and your gut. Gut is the yearning of your soul. It is the longing to make a difference now. It is the way home. The way home is you becoming your grit in the second half of life.

As we work through the Discover process in the Designing Your Encore Life Package, it is not only important to understand passion and purpose, but it is also important to understand limiting beliefs that get in the way of finding passion and purpose. Limiting beliefs for women in the second half of life tend to fall into two categories. One is the idea that we are not enough. The other is that we need to follow the 'Shoulds' that have been programmed in our minds. When we are young, we receive messages about who we are, who we are as girls, who we are as individuals, and who we are as an ethnic identity. Our identity becomes a product of our experience. As a girl my identity was wrapped up in being a preacher's kid in a family where fit and love were missing-at least for me. My identity was built around the need for love, attention, and normalcy. I didn't get the love, attention, or stability I wanted and needed, so I learned ways to get it for myself. I was a shy girl who had a way with teachers. I was an eager learner and pleaser. My favorite elementary school memory was as a third grader. I had pneumonia and had to stay at home in bed for a month under a steam tent. I hated every moment of my life. When I was finally able to go back to school, as I walked through the door, late as usual, my teacher stood up and started to clap. Then, all the students stood up to follow her lead. This was a pivot point for me. I decided that just maybe I was good enough. Now, as a woman in the second half of life, I still need love, attention, and stability. I see that the right motivation is to love myself. I see that as women, now in later life, we must help each other love ourselves and send the message that we are all enough. We show that we are enough in the way we care for our relationships. We show we are enough in the way we care for our families. We know we are enough in the way we manage our work and family life. Women are the bringers of joy. Women are the bringers of love and women are the bringers of hope. Now, in the second half of life we must continue our roles as bringers of hope, while at the same time giving ourselves a pat on the pack for being more than enough.

As I think about life now, I think that we must all choose to be enough. Not feeling enough is a primary cause of our pain. Not feeling enough is a primary cause of conflict. When we truly love ourselves, we don't need the approval of others. When we truly love ourselves, we can give our love away. When I feel enough, I can see that you are enough. We can then rise together, and the world becomes a better place.

The 'Shoulds' of life come from early programming about who we are as females and how we should be as females. As women, we have been programmed to feel responsible for others happiness. We have been programmed to feel less than because we are women. And, we have been programmed to carry the burdens of family life. Shedding the 'Shoulds' of our early programming is the way to find peace in later life. The only 'Should' I recommend we hold onto to, is that we should love ourselves. We should love ourselves enough to love others for who they are and let go of expectations about how we think they should be. Freedom is feeling free from 'Shoulds'. What 'Shoulds' is roaming around in your mind? What 'Shoulds' need to be shed?

Summary: Discover is the process of determining and deciding who you want to be as a 'Master' in your second half of life. Discover is the process of uncovering your limiting beliefs that may get in the way of true self-discovery. Discover is diving deep to explore strengths, values, and passions that define the YOU, you want to be in later life. Discover is the process that helps you get to Your Best Self, Living Your Best Life NOW. Getting to Your Best Self and Living Your Best Life for the greater good is becoming your grit.

Step 2: Define- What You Want to Do

Define is the step where the 'True You' decides who she wants to be and why she wants to be different now. It is the step where all of the Discover elements of the 'True Me' get narrowed down to the 'Essential Me'. It is the time where 'Essential Me' gets to say goodbye to the limiting beliefs and 'Shoulds' in a way that frees the 'Essential Me' to design forward unrestricted. Define is about shedding your 'Shoulds' and choosing your 'Musts' in the second half of life.

What is a 'Must'? A 'Must' is who we are and what we believe at our deepest, most authentic self. It is what calls to you now. It's our passions, our convictions, our urges, and desires. My approach takes you through a process of deciding your 'Musts' to arrive at the core words and phrases that inform a Vision Statement that follows the sequence of 'True Me' –'Wants To'- 'So That'. This Encore Life Vision Statement becomes the condensed version of your idea of you as Your Best Self, Living Your Best Life NOW in the second half of life. As I developed and personally worked through the Designer's Way process, I arrived at the following 'Must' words:

- **'True Me':** Designer, fun-loving, grit, changemaker, compassionate

- **'Wants To':** Empower, connect, play, design, explore

- **'So That':** Difference, meaning, happy, love, soul

These words became the drivers for my **Encore Life Vision Statement**, which is:

As a woman in the second half of life, I intend to engage my independent, adventuresome, compassionate, visionary, and wise self to empower women and girls to discover, design, and manifest a life that reaches true potential regardless of age. In addition, I intend to travel for pleasure and purpose, connect with like-minded women, cherish, support, and play with loved ones, and stay active and healthy so that I can continue to make a difference and rock the retirement years for good.

Defining is the step that empowers dreaming. Defining is the step that gives dreaming some structure so that dreaming can become reality.

Summary: Define is you deciding who you want to be now. Define is narrowing down all possibilities to get to the few 'Must' words that describe what the 'True You' wants to do now as a woman in the second half of life. Define culminates in an Encore Life or Encore Career Vision Statement.

Step 3: Dream- Imagine All Things Possible

Dreaming is the step for fantasy making. Dreaming is taking your Encore Life or Encore Career Vision Statement on a ride to all things possible. Dreaming is shedding your 'Shoulds' and letting your imagination fly. Dreaming is taking away all limitations to empower unrestricted ideation. Dreaming is getting out of your way to find your way. Dreaming happens when you think of all the ways your Vision Statement can play out. Take sticky posts and write all the ways your Vision Statement could become a reality. Don't let limiting beliefs or conditions get in the way. When we allow ourselves to dream big, we can discover new ways to work, play, connect, and be healthy in ways not thought of before.

I think it is important to make dreaming a part of your everyday life. As an INFP, my feeler side likes to dream about ways to use my design thinking skills for social innovation. I want to continue to connect with like-minded people in ways that make a difference. I want to help others to continue to dream their dreams. As I grow my business, I give a portion of my profits to help under privileged children dream their dreams. These HALO Girls are the girls that come from challenging environments but have the ability and drive to become changemakers. I see these girls as critical to the future success of the world. I want to do my part to help challenge become opportunity.

Summary: Dream is about setting free your imagination. It is about letting go of limiting beliefs to imagine all possibilities that may not have been considered before. Dreaming is connecting to your 'True Self' to imagine all ways possible.

Step 4: Decide- Move into Action

Now is the time for discernment. Now is the time for deciding what your 'True Self' wants to do. Now is the time to decide what doing looks like in the areas of: health and wellness; love and relationships; work and service; adventure and play. Now is the time to prioritize ideas, narrow down options, choose the path forward, and make a plan to get there. The Design Thinking process works to arrive at BDOs. BDOs stand for Best Doable Options. Best Doable Options are ones that are reality based now. I arrived at four BDOs, one for each of the work, love, health, and play areas. These are:

- Explore and plan relationship and family adventures

- Become a Life Coach

- Continue my health and fitness program

- Create a way to connect with like-mined women in a way that empowers girls

I have a goal to continue to explore the world with my guy. I have a goal to make some lasting new memories with my family. I have a goal to continue to stay at my current level of fitness. I have a goal to develop relations with like-minded women by creating a giving circle that supports my passion for HALO Girls becoming leaders and changemakers. Finally, I have launched my own Life Coaching Model which is an Online Designing Your Encore Life 'Design and Do' Lab. I arrived at these BDOs by choosing my 'Musts' for each of the areas listed above relating to my Encore Life Vision Statement. I then forced myself to select just one 'Must' for each BDO area.

Once we know our BDOs, it's time to set SMART Goals. SMART stands for Specific, Measurable, Achievable, Realistic, and Time Specific. I encourage clients to set 12-month SMART Goals for each of their chosen BDOs. Next, you can set 3-month SMART Action Steps for each of the SMART Goals. Find a way to hold yourself accountable to these action steps. One idea is to set a regular meeting time with an accountability team of a couple close friends or family members.

Summary: Decide is the process of you narrowing down all possible ides to get to Best Doable Options. It is looking at who you want to be now and making decisions about goals that are not only important, but doable. Design Thinking calls these BDOs. What are the BDOs/Goals that fit your Encore Life or Encore Career Vision Statement that can be achieved in the next 12 months, is the question you want to ask yourself.

Step 5: Develop- Where Action Meets the Road to Reality

Now that you have created an Action Plan, it's time to make your plan become reality. It's time to give your plan the opportunity to succeed. This looks like creating work habits that become life habits. For instance, I am working to create a habit of exercise. I am working to create a habit of doing social media every day and I am making a habit of reflection and writing every day. I am expecting these habits to transform my second half of life. Now that I am working to become my best self, I am wanting to make sure that this best self has a best life to live.

Summary: Develop is the step where action meets the road. It is the step where action becomes life habits.

Step 6: Dance- Reality Making

Dance is the step where new habits become your new reality. Dance is the step where your thoughts attract change. New thoughts about who you are and who you have become will create the energy vibration to achieve your goals. This happens as you create new energy waves as you think about your new life coming to fruition. Dance is you becoming the 'True You'. Dance is you becoming the 'Core You'. Dance is you becoming the howling of your soul. Dance is you becoming your grit.

Summary: Dance is you becoming your true self, your authentic self in a way that gives personality, passion, potential, and purpose new meaning. Dance is your Encore Vision coming to life.

Becoming Your New Reality

Once you've completed the Designing Your Encore Life Package, you'll arrive at an Encore Life or an Encore Career Plan to drive your Encore Performance. Achieving this plan requires creating the mindset to attract your new reality. Achieving the right mindset means creating the right brain wave or energy pattern. Beta waves are slow waves that can attract good outcomes. Theta waves are rapid brain waves that can attract negative outcomes. Working to get into a state of Beta waves is the goal that makes Law of Attraction work in your favor. Becoming means getting into a practice of creating Beta waves.

Suggestions for Growing Your Mindset:

1. Decide that you are on your way to becoming the dream and expect it to happen.

2. Develop a meditation practice that connects thoughts about your new vision with feelings of achievement to create a new lower frequency neuro thought pattern.

3. Develop a habit of play.

Becoming Enough

As women in the second half of life, we have come along way. We have evolved in ways the world has needed us to evolve. We are more independent. We are more educated. We are more interested and invested in the soul of our country. We have become advocates and leaders. We have become thought changers. But somehow, no matter what we accomplish, it never seems enough. We women suffer from the chronic disease of never enough. I am afflicted as well, but I am finally deciding that I am enough. Enough is accepting the real you. When you accept who you are at your core nature, you can begin to love who you are at your core. I get how simple this sounds, but most of us don't accept this premise. Most of us have a neuro thought pattern/habit that continues to tell us that we are just not good enough. My mission is to help women connect with their inner strength and find the courage to become their grit in ways that claim the belief that we are all good enough. We are all on a journey to feel good enough. We are all on a journey to become who we are at our core nature. I am accepting that my core nature has beautiful aspects, and I am accepting that my core nature has difficult aspects and that somehow the package is good enough. Now is your time to look inside to discover the part of you that is not part of your core nature. It is the insecure you that needs to find ways to get approval. This is where Mastery comes in. When you master your 'True Self', you approve of yourself. When you approve of yourself you master life. Mastering life means knowing and accepting that you are enough. You knowing that you are enough gives permission for others to know they are enough. If we feel good enough in the second half of life, we can give ourselves away in ways that we might not otherwise. When we come to a place of enough, we can come to a place of peace. We can accept life as it comes at us. We can accept who we are and where we are in life. Feeling good enough is the path to happy in the second half of life.

Suggestions for Becoming Enough:

1. Accept that feeling not enough is a neuro thought habit. Work to break it by writing down negative thoughts about not being enough. When you are feeling not enough, write your thoughts down without thought or analysis-just write and then immediately throw the paper away. Do this several times a day and watch your mindset change.

2. Feeling not enough is also an attitude about women being inferior to men. Know and accept that we are equal and that the world needs us to feel equal. Remember that women in the second half of life have a biological advantage towards Active Mastery.

3. Go the extra mile in helping others feel good enough.

Becoming Your Own Master- Discernment

I am on my way to becoming my own master. A master is living the life your soul intended. Living the life your soul intended is living your Passion, Purpose, and Power NOW. When you find what Passion, Purpose, and Power looks like for you in the second half of life, you can design your way to happy.

The process of discernment is the process of making decisions. Each of us has our own way of deciding who and what we want to be and what we want to do. My Online 'Design and Do' Lab process starts with collecting Power Words, which are narrowed down to 'Must' Words. We can also use more traditional approaches like considering Pros and Cons. Once I attended a workshop which gave a training in what they called 'So That' Thinking. This thinking process starts with an initial goal like HALO Girls get high quality early education 'So That'......'So That'.....'So That'.....'So That'..... until you arrive at the end 'So That' Goal which might be: They become leaders and change makers. Each of the 'So Thats' become goals to achieve along the way. Now I use this regularly in my decision-making process.

Another way to assess your decisions is to apply discernment questioning. Ask yourself these questions:

- How does the decision feel in my body?

- How does the decision feel in my mind?

- How does the decision feel in my heart?

- How will this decision feel to others who might be impacted by it?

Masters of life are masters of discernment.

Suggestions for Becoming Your Own Master:

1. When you come to a place where you think you have made a decision, test it out.

2. When you decide what is right for you, make sure it is right for others.

3. When you make a mistake, decide there is opportunity to learn from it and find a way to go forward. Failing forward is a critical principle in Design Thinking.

Becoming Free in the Second Half of Life

Freedom is an obtuse concept. Freedom means having the ability and power to allow your thoughts about challenge and change to become your guiding light. Challenge and change bring you the opportunity to know your spirit. I have lived through many life challenges. It's during these times that my spirit has been revealed in ways that show up as grit. Grit empowers the inner strength of my character and I grow because of challenge and not in spite of it. We all have the choice to reframe challenge to see opportunity. When you see opportunity in challenge you see your spirit. When you see your spirit, you come to know freedom. When you know freedom, you see you – the true you.

Freedom is my favorite word. Freedom is what gives meaning to the word power. When you feel free to become the me you want to be, you get to know and understand power. Power is freedom put to good use.

Suggestions for Becoming Free in the Second Half of Life:

1. When challenge comes to visit, stop and work to reframe what has happened. Dig deep to find a way to view this challenge as an opportunity to grow. Think of one thing you can do now to move towards this potential for growth.

2. Make a resolution to find ways to use your personality, passion, potential, and purpose in new ways that give challenge the chance to become opportunity.

Becoming Powerful in the Second Half of Life

I am not interested in power as an ability to control others. I am only interested in power as an expression of who I am and what I love. What you love brings you power in a way that becomes an expression of you. You loving yourself gives you the power to love and help others. As I have watched events play out in America, I am aware of how power corrupts. Power attached to ego is power corrupting, but power attached to heart is power helping. Power attached to heart reflects a connection to personal strengths. When I know and understand my personal strengths, I can have confidence and courage to share them through my heart. Finding and understanding your strengths is the best way to start rethinking how you want to become powerful in the second half of life. One way is to take the Strong Campbell Strengths Inventory. It will give you information about your skills, abilities, talents, and values and then tie this information to possible activity. Connecting your Personality Type with your Strength Inventory brings you to a good place to begin to ideate a new vision for the rest of your life.

Power is also found in forgiving. When you forgive others for transgressions, you release negative energy that impacts you feeling powerful. This doesn't seem to make sense at first glance but feeling angry raises your energy vibration and attracts more negative behavior and outcomes. Forgiving others and releasing blame lowers the energy vibration and attracts better outcomes. Better outcomes help you feel powerful in a good way, not an ego way, which gives you the vibration to keep attracting positive outcomes.

Suggestions for Becoming Powerful:

1. Reconnect with your 'True Self'. Review your Encore vision Statement and Feel the powerful woman that lives there.

2. Find ways to exercise your power. Find causes you care about and get involved.

3. If you find yourself angry and resentful, find the power to forgive. If you find yourself discouraged find your power to help someone else. Find your power in how you love. Love is power. Love is powerful.

Becoming your Grit as a Woman in the Second Half of Life

Grit is power becoming. Grit is you having the courage to own your power in a way that reflects your true character. Character is who you are at your core. Who you are at your core is a woman in the second half of life who wants to continue to make a difference. Making a difference is you becoming your grit in a way that feels powerful.

I am a woman in the second half of life who has arrived through grit. I have experienced and endured many challenges and heartaches, but I have survived through the grit of my spirit. My spirit is grounded as a deep feeler. It is also grounded as a big picture thinker that connects ideas, concepts, and information in unique ways. My spirit reacts to put love first. My spirit has a longing to know itself in new ways now. This new way will always be directed towards helping others find and know their grit. To this end, I hope to start a Girls with Grit Alliance that brings women with grit together in support of HALO (high ability, low opportunity) girls with the grit to become leaders and changemakers. I hope to have the grit to make this happen. If you are interested in this topic, watch for a new guidebook I am producing entitled The Designer's Way: Girls Becoming Their Grit which should be available in early fall of 2021.

Suggestions for Becoming Your Grit:

1. Take stock of your uniqueness. What makes you different? Who is the YOU that hasn't come forward yet?

2. Find ways for the unique you to come out and play. Play is you being yourself doing what you love. Play is you finding Passion, Purpose, and Power NOW as a woman in the second half of life. Play is you at work doing what you love. Play is you with like-minded people talking about what you love to talk about, and play

is you engaging life in ways that makes you feel happy. Grit is you finding ways to make life feel like play.

3. Grit is you being you in a new way that reflects a strength you didn't realize you had. Take the VIA Strength Inventory and pick out an underused and desired strength and figure out a way to use it.

Becoming the Designer of the Rest of your Life

Life design is an ongoing process. As the Designer of the Designer's Way, I see continuing to iterate the steps of Discover, Define, Dream, Decide, Develop, and Dance through the rest of your life as the way to living happily ever after. To me this looks like:

- **Discover:** Continuing to find ways to connect with your 'True Self' so that your soul feels free to fly. It means continuing the work on uncovering and discovering you as your best self. It means continuing the process of shedding 'Shoulds' and limiting beliefs that are getting in the way of you living your best life.

- **Define:** Continuing to work to define what is important to you now. Taking time to decide who you want to be in times of challenge and transition. Taking time to discern how you want to be with the people you are sharing your life with. Taking time to define what meaning and purpose looks like to you as you continue on your journey through life. As we get to our place of understanding and deciding who we want to be and what we want to do, another decision I suggest we make is to decide that good is better than great. In my opinion, great is an ego statement that means we need to be better than. Good is a heart statement that connects accomplishment with helping others. Doing good is great.

- **Dream:** I love the quote by Gabriel Garcia Marquez "We don't stop pursuing dreams because we grow old, we grow old because we stop pursuing dreams". One question to ask is, if life had no limitations of any kind, material or mental, what would your fantasy life be? Try to match a piece of the fantasy life in your head with a calling in the heart and go for it. Create the energy to manifest this dream and watch it materialize. Take time every day to dream and listen to the howling of your heart. I love the idea of dreaming my way home. Dreaming becomes my way of connecting to the other side. I am learning that dreaming is my way of connecting with my higher self.

- **Decide:** Continuing the process of discernment helps clear the path of debris that gets in the way of happiness. Asking yourself the questions: How does this decision feel in my body? How does this decision feel in my mind? How does this decision feel in my heart? How does this decision impact others? This will continue to help you discern your way to happiness and success.

- **Develop:** The ongoing process of taking the time to plan and execute goals and action steps that guide the achievement of the outcomes you want to see. Develop is you finding a way to be accountable to yourself. Creating a support group of friends who will help support, problem solve, and hold you accountable to your plan, is one good way to keep the Life Design process going.

- **Dance**: Dance is you connecting with your higher self in a way that keeps the Designer's Way process alive for the rest of your life. Dance is you living your grit as a woman in the second half of life. Living your grit as a woman in the second half of life is dancing with your spirit to the finish line of life. Dance is believing the finish line is just a new beginning.

Suggestions for Becoming the Designer of the Rest of Your Life

1. Find ways to replace the goal of great and trade it in for the goal of good. What does good look like to you now and how can you do good now?

2. Get out of your own way. Dance. Dance. Dance. The world will dance with you.

To learn more and to purchase the Designing Your Encore Life Package, visit encoredesignherlife.com and begin the Journey Back To YOU, the 'True You' that wants to become her grit in the second half of life.

Sources:

- Burnett, Bill and Evans, Dave, "Designing Your Work Life", Alfred A. Knopf, New York, 2020

- Dispenza, Joe, Dr. "Breaking the Habit of Being Yourself", Hayhouse, 2012

- Alboher, Marci, "Encore Career Handbook", Workman Publishing, 2013

- Luna, Elle, "The Crossroads of Should and Must", Workman Publishing, 2015

- Braun Levine, Suzanne, "Inventing the Rest of Your Life", Penguin Group, 2005

- Burnett, Bill and Evans, Dave, "Designing Your Life", Alfred A. Knopf, New Your 2016

- Gail Rentsch and The Transition Network, "Smart Women Don't Retire, They Break Free, Springboard Press, 2008

- Hanscom, David, MD. "Back in Control" Vertus Press, 2016

- Jackson, Mike MS. MFT, "Natural Differences and the Healing Process", Natural Personality Institute

- Coon, Anne C. and Feuerherm, Praeger, 2017

Printed in the United States
By Bookmasters